salmonpoetry

Nest

Ed Madden

Published in 2014 by
Salmon Poetry
Cliffs of Moher, County Clare, Ireland
Website: www.salmonpoetry.com
Email: info@salmonpoetry.com

ISBN 978-1-908836-63-2

COVER IMAGE: *Cardinal's Nest, Late Autumn* by Mitchell Lonas –
http://mitchelllonas.com.
COVER DESIGN & TYPESETTING: *Siobhán Hutson*
Printed in Ireland by Sprint Print

For Bert

Yea, the sparrow hath found an house,
and the swallow a nest.

PSALM 84:3

Contents

IV

I

Inferno

rice field, Cowlake, Arkansas, 1980

Hell appeared when Ben sat on the levee,
and the outer darkness opened up behind him.
Before then, it did not exist, or existed

only as the story of a rich man, thirsty,
wanting a poor man to dip the tip
of his finger in water and cool his tongue.

Some summers before, I stumbled up
when the church sang my name—*o sinner*—
up for the dunking, preventative, like dipping sheep,

or dogs. Dogs licked the poor man's sores.
O taste and see, says the psalm—meaning
the tongue is how we know the world—

and then God with his footbaths and sheep dip,
God with his crop dusters, sowing love
and death, the bitter grains of it trickling

down my shirt, burning, God with his levees
and me with my shovel, digging a spillway
in the levee for the water to come later,

and Ben sitting there, his jeans ripped
at the knees, the crotch, watching me,
the darkness opening up behind him. The rice

was coming up all over, like a green
fuzz, like hair. I didn't look. I did.
There will be weeping and gnashing of teeth.

The fire is not quenched, the worm does not die.
The tongue is also a fire. It defiles
the whole body. The crop dusters are flying

over. Ben is not a metaphor. The field
is hot. There's a water jug in the truck.
Oh, that he would dip the tip of his finger

in water and cool my tongue.

Among men

farm shop, Cowlake, Arkansas, 1974

The rain beats insistent
against the shop's walls, the men

stand around the stove
or sit, or lean over to spit

in the plastic bucket,
the slung string of it, fragrant

and chewed, and butts fizzled
in the brown pool. One man

cuts hair, a boy stuck there
while the men talk

or don't, hands shaping the air
around his head, comb and

old scissors mincing around
his ears. He stares into the stove,

one of those with gas flames
licking the broken grates—

ornate radiants glowing
and broken, bright combs maybe

for some devil's honey.

Wrestling / Fable with shag carpet and bean bag chairs

In this corner: my brother, grinning.
In that: my young uncle, flexing.

After dinner, time for the games.

In an arena bounded by sofa
and window, by our parents

listening from the kitchen,

we mimicked moves we'd seen on tv,
standards of spandex and skin,

boys learning the throw and pin.

This was before the den's deep swank,
its shag, its fireplace, its beanbag chairs.

This was before sin.

On this side: light. On this side:
darkness. Between them

the lunge, the chokehold.

Tagged, I'd take my place in the ring,
take my stand, my stance,

assume the position.

I could never escape, pinned
and wriggling like that,

pinned to the mat.

This was before Little League football,
before the house burning down,

before *The Clue in the Embers.*

In this corner: a boy who will win.
In this corner: a boy who will lose.

Family Bible

my yoke is easy, my burden is light

Names in layers between testaments,
weight of pages, thick sediment—

and all the scripture closing in. I'd run
a finger down the lists to the one:

my name, a boy beneath so many dead.

Not ready yet for the heft of red letters,
real leather, my own little bible was zippered,

with pictures, easy to read and light.
Till the night I stepped to the aisle—

stunned by the heat, the maudlin song,
the beat of the preacher's speech, the long walk,

fire-and-brimstone talk, choral roar
of Jesus calling, and a hand firm on my shoulder

pushed me back into the water. And I was raised,
they said, raised from the grave—*saved*—

the white robe, grave-clothes, heavy, wet, and cold.

Dragonfly, beetle

summer 1971

Were it not for the rice field; were it not
for the fact that you are here under this sun,
alone, leaning across a levee; were it not

for your anger at your brother, walking
the road away from him and your cousins,
playing war or whatever, the smart of what

would become rejection, you would never
have known this small violence, so visible,
now, in the flow of water along the levee,

the larva of the diving beetle. Its hooked jaws
hold some smaller creature, a tadpole,
a worm—you can't remember now—just

those pincered jaws, the sun on your neck,
the day quiet but for the wind in the rice,
a dragonfly glistening on a thin leaf, the field

spread out before you, no longer a field, but
a world of submerged violence, small, quiet,
the hook of hunger, the desperate writhing.

Larval

Housed in a mayonnaise jar, ice-picked lid. I fed it lettuce,
drops of water like dew. It never grew, just shat black bits.

I cleaned the jar, let it crawl my arm: tickle of worm,
wooly bear, soft-bodied prickle, sticky thing.

It reared at the tip of my index, thorax lifted, felt
for the needed link-limb-finger, branch to catch. I left

a stick stuck against the lid, hoped to see a lynch
of silk. Never did. Grew bored. The jar smelled sour.

The caterpillar slowed, fuzzy slug, bit of latent guilt—
a bubble of brown vomit at its mouth.

Nest

Dark wings flickered at the eaves,
wasps circled the barn, dirt-daubers'
knobbed nests like clods chunked and lodged

along the beams, eggs packed inside,
nestled beside tiny spiders, stung,
paralyzed. Time doesn't heal. No

emotion is the final one. The yellow jackets
sabotaged the toolbox, the unhooked plow,
the diesel tank, the gate, their paper nests

like pale morels hung to dry, and red wasps
throbbed like bunched explosives just above
our heads—the barn seethed with the sound,

we felt it like static on our skin, their nests
I-dare-you's for any boy. Black daubers flashed
and dabbled at the field's last puddles,

the fish-gasping ditch, chewing bits of mud.
Once again, we assumed the adults around us
knew what they were doing, the wasps sealing

their young up with the spiders, stung,
paralyzed, ready to be eaten alive.

Genealogy: unidentified man in a photograph

There had been a bachelor uncle, perhaps,
or something no one ever talked about:
incidents of betrayal and revenge, a wedding
that never happened, or one that did, the way
they did, the way such stories always ended.
Perhaps a baptism in the muddy river nearby.

It had to be hard then, so hard to get by,
to know the curve of a man's face, the bristled
chin, the burning eyes. Someone's mother
had been involved in some way. They were
unbending back then, as if they were made
of something stronger than human stuff. The flesh

is weak, but the spirit is strong. So he would live
the best that he knew how. Before the fall,
before redemption, there had been moments
of such intensity that he had no words,
no language, only the burning. All flesh is grass,
the scent of mown fields, of wheat stubble

burning in the distance. How can I tell
the story now: assemble the fading photos,
the journal with pages missing, the genealogy
spreading like roots in the family bible,
which survived two floods, a fire—history
rescued from the flames. There is a small box

with a lock of hair, a clay marble. Examine
these things. Tell the story not recorded.
Notice the man at the edge of the photo, his smile,
his burning eyes, his hands behind his back,
as if he is holding something, or withholding
something, the family attentive only to the camera,

the grass of the yard beaten down
into a smooth and empty page.

Dead

My father and uncle helped me undress.

I left my daily clothes on a desk
in the classroom, and they helped me into a robe

that smelled of chlorine and dust. Someone

was singing, I could hear it—
O happy day, that fixed my choice—

beyond the closed doors, the empty halls.

They helped me down the dark slick stairs
to where he waited, watching me, to where

the man in rolled-up sleeves took me in his arms,

pressed his left hand against the small of my back, his right
over my nose and mouth, then dipped me

as in a dance, pushed me under

the water and held me there—buried with him,
raised a new man—that's what they said.

When I woke I was shivering.

When I woke, I was dead, or
instead, I left the dead man there, in the water.

Or I was alive and the dead man held me
like a shadow, sometimes rising before me,

standing on my feet like a child,

sometimes stretching behind
to touch that man in the rolled-up sleeves,

waiting there in the dark water,
in the corner where the ripples pushed

as I descended into the rafts of insects,
litter of dead things.

When I left

When I left I was dead.
When I left, my father mourned me every day.

When I left, the oak trees held their dead leaves,
scattered acorns across the lawn like hard tears,

hard like what my father said over scrambled eggs
in the hospital cafeteria, and later,

as I rehearsed it in my head.
The oak trees hold their dead leaves.

The oak tree lifted Absalom up for Joab's love:
for the three spears he thrust in his heart while he hung there,

for the ten young men who came later, for the pit
they cast him in, the heaped stones.

II

Calling

Because I wanted to be a prophet,
I was given a pocket pitchpipe,
round red thing with metal reeds,
and a family that couldn't sing, given

a grandma who left me in the back
room to press flowers in stacks
of old *Reader's Digests*, who gave me
paper and glue and cinnamon toast.

Asked to work with Aunt Maxine
in VBS, I learned the language
of crayon and scissors and flannelgraph,
language of the gold foil stars.

Because I wanted to be a preacher,
I was given a father who didn't
like to read, a mother who did,
a brother who listened to Queen, given

Chronicles of Narnia, anything Tolkien,
the Hardy Boys and Agatha Christie
to teach me there are answers, if you
look—and later a copy of Beckett,

a book in which my mother marked
in red the bad words, bad things.
Given a camera with which I took
too many photos of daylilies and toads.

Given a house at the end of the road.

Because I wasn't to be a prophet,
I was given a prick that wouldn't
stay down, when I sat at the front
at church and a boy touched my leg

and laughed at me when we stood to sing.

Nest

Green pecans litter the street, crushed
and pungent on the hot walk. A hatchling,

just a puff of grey down, shrieks
in the grass, somewhere a nest, and in the west

a promise of storm, the sky gone black.

A shrike eyes the tiny bird, its song
monotonous, it won't shut up, little dollop

of feather, all beak and eyes. The shrike
is quiet. The pasture fence is twisted wire,

here and there barbs beaded
with impaled things.

Playground

Rutherford Elementary, 1969

When Mark Nicholson spilled his milk on me—a slosh
across my lap—the teacher let me tip the rest
on him, then slipped me in some spare jeans in her closet,
and that was that. From then on, *teacher's pet.*

Carroll Toddy fell out the back of a swing that fall,
knocked him out, left a knot on his round head
like a horn. On cold days, our teams devolved
to backwards tag, the boy with the ball running the field,

and all the rest after him—*smear the queer*—trying
to tag or tackle him. No way to win. Tagged, he'd toss
the ball, lob it in the mob of us, or hurl it high—
snag it and *you're it*—scramble past, run cross

the yard. No out of bounds, no teams, no rules,
until the bell called us back inside for school.

Vacation Bible School

Every day, something to make,
something to color, a page to take home.
Later, there'd be store-bought cookies.
Later, there'd be Kool-Aid or punch.

I was Aunt Maxine's helper
for summer Vacation Bible School.
I helped the little girls with stickers.
I helped the little boys with crayons.

Sometimes we'd use glue and glitter,
or make something with tongue depressors.
Later, there might be a puppet lesson.
Later, there'd be prayer and songs.

We'd sing, *Roll the gospel chariot.*
Or, *The B-I-B-L-E.*
Or, *Be careful little tongue.*
Sometimes I got to lead the songs.

I was the boy teacher's helper,
the only boy among the girls.
Sometimes, I'd get to tell the story,
and sometimes use the flannel board.

The men had beards and flowing robes.
Joseph's face was young and smooth.
Joseph's coat was a woven rainbow.
My face was smooth, though not for long.

Church camp, summer 1977

Three boys on the upper bunks
spend an afternoon looking

for dirty stuff in the Bible,
find the newer versions better

than the old. They almost look
like scholars, poring over books,

parsing words like *concupiscence*.

Chosen / Commentary on Psalm 139

I will praise thee: for I am fearfully and wonderfully made.
PSALM 139

I

Rain drums the gym windows, where he sits
on a bench in afternoon PE, sits in the funk
of the junior high locker room—

Thine eyes did see my substance, yet being imperfect—

a boy with feathered hair and buck teeth,
boy with thin wrists and thick glasses,
glasses he sets aside, when Coach Parnell

makes the boys box, when Coach Parnell
chooses him, when Coach Bubba Parnell decides
to pit two skinny near-sighted boys, the two

(the way it was said those days) *sissies—*
For there is not a word in my tongue,
but lo, O Lord, thou knowest it altogether.

II

On the lawn after lunch, he leans on a tree,
reading Hebrews, II Timothy, the epistle
for this week's quiz. He wants to win, wants
to fight the good fight, finish the course,

keep the faith. The world of football and gossip
swirls around him—*so great a cloud of witnesses—*
he is learning to see himself, learning
shame—shame for the way he carries his books,

shame for hand-me-downs and high-waters,
shame for the bone that pops in morning English
and afternoon band, in study hall with Coach Burch
and his thick *Magnum PI* moustache,

where Terri and Cindy pass around *Jaws*
or a raunchy novel about a killer gator
with the juicy bits marked, shame—
that my substance was not hid from thee,

when I was made in secret, and curiously wrought in the lowest parts.

III

To be chosen.
To stand on mats between benches lined with boys.
To strap on the worn red gloves, the warm red gloves.

Do I not hate them, O Lord?

To swing the gloves wildly—*like a girl*—
to keep swinging without seeing.

To feel good—*how good it felt*—
that Billy Cowell's mouth was bloodied by the gloves,
his lip split, his silver braces gleaming and bloody.

Marvelous are thy works; and that my soul knoweth
right, and that my soul knoweth right well.

Jubilate

For I will read queer things in punk magazines in English.
For we will talk about David Bowie and Rod Stewart in art.
For I will watch Sting sing 'Don't stand so close to me' on
    Friday Night Videos
as I lie on a bed in Sheryl Honey's house my senior year,
for I will lie on the bed with Elizabeth, who loaned me the magazines,
for I will lie on the bed with Paul, the quarterback with perfect
    hair and tanned ankles,
for we will watch Sting sing 'Don't stand so close to me.'

Let us rejoice with Rod Stewart, who says
no point in talking when there's nobody listening.
Let us rejoice with Sting, who sings,
don't stand so, don't stand, don't stand.
Copa Cabana, Mama Mia, Amen.

For there is a bar in Oxford called the Jolly Farmer.
Thou knowest my downsitting and mine uprising,
thou understandest my thought afar off.
For there I will meet a man named David,
for we will hear Erasure sing, 'Take a chance on me.'
Such knowledge is too wonderful for me—
For we will wait in line to enter Heaven, where I will dance
    with David—
If I ascend up into heaven, thou art there—
for I will hear a remix of 'Even better than the real thing'
and we will leave together—
if I make my bed in hell, behold thou art there.

For what you do when you are confused
will make you certain.

For what I assume is membership

That was the first party, and all those bodies stippling the carpet,
whispers about a military man, out of uniform, and below us

the dark trails. He touched me on the balcony, asked me if
we could keep each other's secrets—the parsing of all those lies.

The car wouldn't start, I said, or was it the *too-late-to-drive story?*

Later there was that yellow letter, some drivel about love,
a rug, a key to a trunk full of porn, and something about *if I die.*

I told the man from the laundry about it, after he folded his clothes
and we traded massage in a room filled with steam—like any story,

another clunky fiction of seduction. But that was months later.
We leaned on the balcony then, naked, below us the lake's edge

in ruffles of black, bats stitching the dark air, men
on moon-dark paths below, following a sound too fine to hear,

the way my first love turned that day, as if—turned at the corner,
turned and waited.

III

Knowledge

Ireland, May 2006

I.

On the schoolboy's list, the GPO, famed portico,
this row of six stone columns—we check it off, *done*—

Cuchulain and the crow in the window, then the spire—
the stiffie at the Liffey someone says—Parnell, our Joyce

jaunty boyo in a nearby street. Later, after dinner,
I wander back on my own, finger the fluted columns'

grooves, the nicks and knocks, bulleted pocks.

II.

We walked the path up Knocknarea—that knuckle
of rock—a rutted lane dissolving to a trail

over stone and heather, shudder of sheep gates, drizzle
pelting the top. All the way down we named the flowers—

orchid, pennywort, furze, vetch. The rain
came harder. In walls of rock along the bottom lane,

clumps of primrose were glowing between the stones.

III.

A few years back, I met a Wexford gardener in Temple Bar—
shy smile and thick hair, a spurt of it flirting his collar, and,

I'd discover, a filigree of jet on his chest, insular script
embellishing each nip and the rest—*his heart was going like mad*—

mouth sweet with beer and sweat, hard hips in hands,
and in the dark, the shiver and stiffness, the brush and braille

of him—each sweet bud, each cleft, traced with finger, tongue.

Lost islands

for Fran

At dinner it surfaces, that old island of the past—
center of the table, tureen of cioppino, bottles
of red wine—six hours of dinner to get here,

and here we are, edge of the cliff, the waves below.
The glasses have flushed red and white—
and that light burns at the base of the spine.

*

Years later, a late lunch on Inishmore—
oysters that were bits of ocean on the tongue—
rain arrives on the far side of empty sky,

and after, the vertiginous lawn of Dun Aengus
in a cold mist, brink of the sea, and Hy-Brasil
on the horizon—said to vanish if you try to reach it.

*

Every seven years: light the fire, the island stays—
such dry knowledge. What lies beneath, beyond,
what mayhem, what memory, what shift and lift

of cold waves, what drift of bones, what myth
of swans long gone? A woman I'd sworn
to marry sits beside the woman she loves.

Aisling at the Yeats Summer School

Two loves I have of comfort and despair.
SHAKESPEARE

The narrow Sligo streets thickened with secrets,
melodramas of fog, cigarettes and cider
on Helen's lips. We kissed in the dark room,
empty bunks around us, the other boys
having coffee in the adjoining kitchen,
listening. . . . And then he came to me,
walking down Markiewicz, his red hair
and white hands, his knee against mine
under the table at tea one afternoon.
He was fresh off the ferry from France,
an attorney on tour, of Irish descent,
his green eyes glossed with a blue sky's
brightness. The day he left his key and caught me
in the street, asked me to let him in,

we rushed back to find company gathered
in the house. I had two loves of comfort
and deception: Helen's timid fingers
on my hand, his knee against my knee,
rubbing undetectably, that summer
of masks and lies, a man's eyes bright
with revelation—summer of Helen, summer
of a man whose name I can't recall,
just a face, the knee, shoulders broad
in dreams, and my vacillation, refusing
to admit quite yet that I was waiting
for this vision, this deliverance, years
before I would lament the nameless men,
the years lost, what might have been.

Teanga Na mBláthanna /
The language of flowers

Oideas Gael, Glencolmcille, July 2008

In Glencolmcille, I am learning
the name of each flower I find.
The purple spike of foxglove: *lus mór*.

Each morning I say the names
as I walk this little path,
its traffic of sheep and bumblebees,

hedge and fence full of fuchsia—
deora Dé, God's tears—full of gorse,
full of honeysuckle and briar,
bits of wool on the barbed wire.

The pink fist below the bridge
is called *caorthann corraigh*.

Fields of iris, flags—yellow streamers,
yellow flowers all along the road,
orange march, green country.

The swallows interpret the field.
The sheep say *beatha, beatha*—life, life.

I don't know the name for the horsetails.
What is the name for a thistle,
gilded silver with rain?

What is the name for a sunset
flowering on the mountain just before dark?

Saint's finger, Hill of Slane

Almost stepped on it, on them, bits of digit,
a pinky, knuckle, in the grass and gravel, graveside,

no blood, just dust, grit, some wire in it, in them,
the fingers, bits fallen off, but it's the savior

not a leper, or perhaps St. Pat, some pope—don't know,
just that he's mythic, biblical, robed, and old

as these things go, though these tombs are newer than
the ruins all around—the stone he's propped on

a grave of the lately gone— he's chipped, maybe chapped,
grey saint, white-washed, waving his hand

like that, disfigured benediction for those damn kids
crawling the walls and up inside the old tower,

cider and crisps in the friary, butts, some fumbling
about the motte and bailey just beside, relics

left behind, like these knocked off parts
on the lawn, almost stepped on, those two

bent digits in the litter that say he was divine
and not, flesh like us, to be picked up, pocketed.

Shark

In the boat's wake as we leave Slieve Leabh,
sunlight spangles scattered spray, and the boat

slides slow, lee side, toward the cliffs,
precipitous dip of wave and wing, great slopes

of stone, the crash of things, and just as we veer
back out, the basker's lazy fin pulls us

in, again, limp knife slicing the waves,
flip of dorsal flap but still a shark,

the gold brown length of it just below us,
beside the boat, and close enough to see

the huge mouth agape—open and glowing,
filter and gill, combing for krill with—

céad míle fáilte—a hundred thousand teeth.

Without

I. Dun Aengus

for Jessie

Close sky and cliffs,
a skiff of cloud, gull-cry,

wind, and out there,
somewhere, my friend,

the wave-lashed rocks.
Fog-locked, mist-washed,

I'd crawl the ledge,
edge my way across,

shimmy over, shoulder-ease
and knee-tremor and shiver.

I'd take my glasses off to see
the sea, make myself look

down. I remember it,
the rim of it, the sound,

face in the salt spray—
the only way to face it.

II. Round Top

for Jack

I wake here, Texas,
breakfast an hour away,

all knee-creak and bladder,
chigger-itch and needing

coffee. It's already hot out,
cloudy, white poppies

in bloom on the walks.
We talk in the dark room

about our fathers, and loss—
the close dark lets us talk.

At breakfast later
we hear we missed

the early bird walk—
the songs they learned,

what they heard.

Late spring, near Leakey, Texas

This green season comes, in morning's green
light, the sun dangling small and bright
in a green sky—a flash of fin, sunfish
suspended, cool and luminous in the green
water. Everywhere we look, the past—pawprints
at water's edge, trees that keep repeating
themselves, small birds playing hide and seek,
bluffs of rock, striated and grained, remnants
of sediment, pressure. The sun rests on a bluff,
beside a cross someone built, a memorial.
Light drifts across the green water.
We cross the stream, dry our feet, pull on
shoes, roll down our jeans. Here, though nothing
is said, there's a sense of something moving
through us, a sense of water and rock, darkness, light.

Fishing off the Kona coast

Hawaii, June 2005

The coast is a postcard.
Off the starboard,

a pair, a pod of false killers wake-
ride, the black fins, their slick backs

sleek curves glistening in the surf—
and beyond, the white-tailed tropicbirds

cruising the open ocean for flying fish.

*

Flying fish skitter at the bow,
and we steer toward

a thick flutter of shearwaters—
that frenzy a signal of predator

fish, the skipjack driving mackerel
scad to the surface, larval spatter,

feeding frenzy of the dark birds.

*

The rod dips, the line sings, its hum
fills your gut. Your arms

tremble. On the slick deck,
plant your butt against the thick

arm of the fighting chair. Lift
the rod, quick reel as you dip it, lift

and reel, feel the pull,
use your hips to lift and reel until

it's part of you—your wrist will keep
reeling in sleep—

*

You reel until someone sees it—
metallic and bright in the blue deep—

scramble of men to the stern—
keep reeling! Knee braced you lean

to see it—not yet landed, just that flash,
that silver flash when the sun catches it—

that moment.

Field Guides, Big Island

I. Kohala

At the fish and chips shop, we stop
and watch the green pond. The water boils

with koi, and when our food comes, we flip
fries in the water, bits of oyster

and batter—doesn't matter what, they'll eat it.
Two teens toss their cups of ice,

a frenzy of fish mouthing the cold globes.

II. Ka'u

On a trail through the *Kipuka Pua'ulu*—
island of old growth spared by the lava flows—

we stop, stunned by a brawl of kaliij pheasants
on the walk, two cocks and a scatter of hens.

Later a birder says they're just imports
taking over the park, above us the *apapane*,

chubby honeycreeper, singing in the old trees.

III. Puna

Water batters the lava cliff. Beneath
our shoes we feel the crunch of tiny shells—

the littorines and nerites that crust
the rock, pimples of black, *grain de plomb*.

Just beyond us, a comma of black sand,
a spatter of children. We look up to see

a thin mongoose scurry behind the showers.

At a greenhouse in Kona Kai

Big Island, Hawaii, July 2005

The front walk is lined with protea—honeypot
and sugarbush, these horny, stalked things, tight
fists of flower. And among the epiphytes,
the night-blooming cereus sprawls from its pot

like a drunk, white slugs of bloom spent
and fallen in the thick grass. The walk
beneath the trees is hot, filled with dark
afternoon light, the fertile scents

of plumeria and dirt. The trees screen
the sea. A tangle of flat, fleshy leaves
extends along a beam in the low eaves
of the greenhouse—the tender, pendulous beans

of vanilla. A man smiles at the bell's summons,
his bare chest dusted with hair like pollen.

Tenantry

As if the yard
were really ours
and not just four years

of gardening
someone else's plot—
this small family
of ceramic pots.

On a postcard of the old Dublin airport

What was up-to-date about
this place eludes us, but look: the dull

horizon is a flag—green
field, white hanger, orange

gates. Oh, and that red plane—
a toy to hurl into the future.

IV

To get to Cowlake

To get to Cowlake, look for a gravel road,
barely wide enough for two pickup trucks—

you'll have to back up if a backhoe or combine
is coming through. Ignore all the signs,

which say Amagon, Algoa, Beedeville, Balch,
Grubbs, Remmel, maybe Marked Tree.

Turn left if coming from Oil Trough, right
if you're coming from McCrory, where you took

Granny Lola to the doctor one summer
when a brown recluse bit her, and if

you're coming from Memphis, always remember Memphis
is the best way out. To get to Cowlake, pretend

you're driving a '76 bird's-egg blue Ford
truck, spit cup wedged against the dash,

seed cap on the seat. To get to Cowlake,
you need to put on that cap.

You'll pass some well pools and rice fields,
an old home site covered in careless weed,

the trailer where your cousin Tony lives.
Some days, crop-duster wake may lead you

there, bittersweet scents of fertilizer
and herbicide, of growing and dead things.

When you get to the old WPA road marker,
just before Uncle Herv's, turn right—

a sharp turn, deep ditches on each side.
Name the trees: the osage orange, which is

Uncle Ralph's driveway; the weeping willow
on the hill, which is Uncle Dale's yard,

across from the cemetery; the catalpa tree
in Granny Lola's horse pasture, bearing

its annual crop of worms. Don't look for a church.
It's no longer there, just a bare yard,

a small grain bin, a shed. To get to Cowlake,
don't look for cows or a lake. There are no cows.

Sometimes, though, the creek floods.

Nest

19 June 2011

Two buds on the stargazer lily.
Three blue eggs in the tiny nest—

unlikely spot, tucked under the gauge
of the carport air compressor,

someplace a snake can't climb,
or cat, someplace safe,

despite the human traffic this weekend,
as mourners drop by to see my mom.

I lift my niece to see the bird
on the nest, its tiny black eyes

looking back at us, around us the blue
mud daubers flashing their blue-black wings.

Coon Island: two poems

after Seamus Heaney, in memory of my father

1. Rose of Sharon

There was a sunlit absence,
a chill despite the sun up
and the hot wind,
the hyacinths sunk

back into the grass,
and the daffodils—
the bulbs he dozed
across the yard

with a bushhog—gone too.
So, what was left was just
a Rose of Sharon
no bigger than a weed,

leaning with the weight
of three blooms. She stood
beside it, that June,
in her church clothes.

Now she sits in the quiet
house, or reads, or turns
toward the chair
where he used to sit

and read.
Here is his Bible,
a slip of paper
still marking some verse,

and here is love
like the woodbox stocked
with small logs,
ready for what's ahead.

2. The Angelus

All around the house there are raccoons,
as if their image could deflect the history
of what happened, of whose farms and homes
were here before my grandpa bought the soggy
bottom fields between the backed-up Cache
and the dredged line of Remmel Ditch.
But here above her chair: two peasants, his cap
in his hands, her hands clasped, a church
on the horizon. Between the couple lies
a basket of potatoes, which masks the small
coffin Millet painted over, the skies
dark with hidden loss, the bells that toll
the difference between what we see and know.
Even from this distance, I hear them now.

Still

Galway, fall 2011

I

One leg is lifted as if to step
but not, not yet—neck and beak
are counterweights, and tucked wings,
a heron testing this leak of creek

just off the *abhainn* proper, a sliver
of water they call a river beside
the river, named for a distillery
or maybe nuns, something vaguely

indigenous, like the bird that picks
its way across the gravel, then stiffens,
shiver of water rushing beneath,
cold feet maybe—sees me

as I freeze on the rickety bridge
above, leaning, watching, still,
little river a shimmer beneath me—
or, more likely, fixed on something

below, some sliver of fish, a waver
of light in water, some litter—and then
something waived, let go, it steps
into a different river, I turn

to go, the white sky begins
to sift a thin mist of rain.

II

I'm sleepy when you skype, lean,
relieved, on my hand like that—
cupped chin, the fat girl shot,
propped—little box of me

I see right there on the right,
that spot, your heart. You walk about
as you talk, the house behind
a whirl of light and walls and bits

of a known world, like
a playground merry-go-round,
whirling cups or something, and you
just across from me, the world

revolving round you, unresolved,
but me, leaning, listening, still.

Jewels of Opar

The thick leaves are chartreuse green,
a green rinsed with piss or morning light.
The thin stems hang over the garden's
tended walks, dangling the slight

pink buds, red pods like tiny baubles—
garnet, ruby, chalcedony. They are not
rare, they are not precious. Gardeners
rip out the spent plants, and already the knots

of pale green leaves pattern the loam,
the cracks of the brick walks. When you found
a darker variant in our yard—*talinum
paniculatum*—you carefully mowed around it.

To our neighbors, an unfinished job,
that lank patch of lawn. To you something
precious—the panicled blooms, lobed
leaves, red gems spangling the dark green.

Possum

A thumping under the tub, something
rubbing, something getting settled in.

One morning, we could hear a soft snoring.

Later, in the crawl space beneath the house,
we found warped boards in the floor

where the pipes come in—
and a whiff of something, fluff and dead leaves.

One night we woke to growls and hissing, a fight,
maybe mating. *They have forked penises, you know,*

he said. I thought about that as the growls
subsided, and outside, in the dark,

wild things roamed the yards.

Scavenge

near Pickens, South Carolina

First two, then a third, there in the circle of light,
trash can lids fixed tight—that old word *varmints*
scrambles to tongue, like a word my father might use,
as strange to me now as *dispensation*, or *atone*.

Among the non-believers, in the cold, we develop the rites
of the not quite, of *almost*: seeds of the sweet pea
tamped into wet dirt, an old jar filled with tulips,
or this week in a cabin, blue sky caught in a cathedral

of bare trees, transformed in the lake beyond.
Every morning, we toss bits of breakfast to the fish,
to two geese wintering here. Every afternoon,
crows patrol the porch for anything left behind,

ignore broken crumbs of quartz carried home
from a hike, glimmering in the light, one gilded
with pyrite, fool's gold, Tomorrow we've planned
an early trip out to the local jockey lot, morning

for a flea market hunt, equipped with a tiny flashlight
to check for damage, to read the marks, to sift
for a gift among the possible, the taken-for-granted,
the lost. The raccoons can smell the salmon from dinner.

One night they levered the lids, got in, chewed
to shreds the paper towels imprinted with fish.
When we walk out now, they scatter. Then one
waddles back to the edge of the light and waits.

Weekend

I. Hammock

The hammock frame has cracked in the rain—
keel of wet wood, an unbuilt boat—
still good you say, just needs some glue
and a clamp, but it's too damp to do it

right now, a project for another day.
In the wet grass, some broken glass—
and a gash on your left foot, the heel.
You limp to the steps and inside to the tub,

wash the red slash and dab it with salve,
tamp down the bandage tabs
on wet skin—they'll hold. The day
is damp and cold. We'll go to Lowe's

later. The hammock is furled in the shed.
A dream of leisure dangles in the frame.

II. Chair

Sleek and slick and *très moderne*—a black
chair leaning in the corner of the room—
like something from *Star Trek*, all pleather
and metal, silver base shaped like a plow.

But it smells like old cheese, a faint
funk that blooms when you remove the thick
cushions, a yard sale find left out
in the rain. We don't mind at first,

thinking we can fix it, but pulled back,
the black seat and back reveal only

pressed wood panels, tacky and wet,
a thin plastic sheet—no frame beneath—

nothing firm but the rusted-out brackets.
Nothing will fix its sagging back.

III. Rent

This time that year, it was the big grill
on the deck, the new thrill of a shower
together, sex in the backyard, and a binge
of B-movies on satellite tv—

two weeks of house-sitting for my boyfriend's
boss in the suburbs—and her dogs,
the yippy inside mop and the big lab
outside. Thirty minutes out and miles away

from our dumpy little duplex with bad
plumbing and an ass for a landlord. And now
you're running out to drop off the rent,
and you point out in the afternoon light

something we haven't seen—I haven't shaved—
that my stubble is now speckled with grey.

Early morning, fortieth birthday

Heavy leaves still green the yard,
no yellows yet, nothing brown.
A fuzz of seed dusts the air—
season of sneezing before the freeze,

before the ground grows cold, hard.
Beside the porch, a yellow spider
stitches a web of sticky silks:
cat's cradle dangling a mummy of moth.

A ticklish dark blurs the hedges
the lozenge of moon swoons above—
a slick of light on a bald spot of yard
glistens like spit-shine on old shoes.

At dawn, the birds dither and fret:
frost sugars the lawn.

In the absence of a contract

A field of rings glistens in the pawnshop
like cold wickets on grey lawns—

like shackles fragile and under glass, locked
boxes, pincushions of love and loss. Pawned

white gold lifted, found—the old vows
around the ring ground down, the tux and gown

now dust, names polished away. Second hand,
it fits your hand. *Ecce homo*. He is the man.

Epithalamion

for Bert, 19 March 2005

The old designs bear witness: they are very much like us.
In March we deck the church with calla lilies, stargazers,

bells of Ireland—the green calyces shaped like bells,
the white tongues of flower. You prefer the real

to the silk, the scentless, the faux rose with its dewdrop
of glue. *This is real*, you said—your words a song

filled with longing, and glossed with the dappled half-light
of spring, the shimmer of pale blossoms. Our small drama

of vows becomes another grammar of assent;
this is the renunciation that is affirmation, a form

of happiness that attends a great loss—those fictions
of law and lineage, annals of blood. The Lenten rose

now glows in our garden like a reason—garden
where our hands meet, sensing that sweet decline

into the ordinary, a handful of daffodils from the yard.

Counterpane

after Melville

I wake with counterpane of arm,
thick and warm, across my chest.

You'd almost thought I'd been his wife,
the way he hugged me tight, as though

naught but death could part us now—
this unbecoming bridegroom clasp,

this strip of quilt a sunburnt arm.

Wings

We looked for a body,
though there was nothing

but a brush of grey
down where the bird

slammed the pane,
its ghost traced in grey

dust, wings spread,
an angel. This was proof,

though we remembered, once,
downtown, coming across

a tiny owl at the foot
of the bank tower,

where it fell.

Reunion / List of defunct rugby league clubs

The reunion was my last reunion.
Wiley, the only other member

of the smartass club, had changed his name.
There was the merger and the reversion,

the shutdown to end the league war.
Steve, the bully, apologized to Denny—

matter of fact, said his son's best friend is gay.
Luckily, Beverly had a bottle-opener on her keys.

Every scrum was a heart condition
in animation, the huff of it, the slip of cleat.

The other bullies didn't show up.
Brothers in the past are past brothers.

The tigers merged with the magpies
or the scorpions, we don't remember.

Castleford is unrelated to Castleford.
Gary was across town for the viewing—

his mother died the night before.
My father died the day after.

We gathered together around the cooler
in the trunk of someone's car.

Denny's krewe had crowned him king,
but that was before Katrina.

Someone switched the topic to football,
or moved back to Blackpool, or Grubbs.

Read the names: Clydesdales, Vipers, Invicta.
Every match was a candy tin filled with teeth.

Star

Bert says old folks used to put
a big tin can around the shoots

of the clematis at the mailbox,
a tube of cool wet dirt at the roots,

those dark blue blooms burning
like stars down that Mississippi

road, over the manger of each
mailbox, cool despite the heat.

An Old Pew

for Ray

He wanted the God of the flannelgraph, God of the box of crayons, God of grape kool-aid and stale cookies, God of the paper tabernacle, God of the quiz bowl, God of the gold star, God of Aunt Maxine and Uncle Doug.

He got God of the tent meeting, the gospel revival, God of the cold immersion, God of the burning cross, God of *Must the Young Die Too?*, God of Brother Wyatt, God of the funeral flowers, God of the last verse, sung once again, for the lost, for the sinners, for the unsaved that remain out there— *yes, you know who you are.*

He wanted a song of the pitchpipe, song of the Rich Old King, song of the red and yellow black and white, song of clap your hands, song of stomp your feet, song of the happy shout, the song sung in rounds.

He heard the altar call song, the invitation song, the revival song, song about a fount of blood, song of the roll call and the last trumpet, song of being blind, song of sinking deep, song of the deep stain, song of the worm.

*

Let there be a song for the man who doesn't sing.

Let there be a song for the man who walks away, song of the dark hand, song of the wandering feet, song of the unsung.

Let there be a god of the night bloom, god of the guestroom, god of the quince and winter wheat, god of last call and first guess, god of the frozen drink, god of the hairy chest, god of the road trip, god of the home-grown, god of the homeward and homely, god of the shared home, a repurposed god, god of the unsaid, god of the old pew at the foot of the bed.

Acknowledgements

Grateful acknowledgement is made to the editors of the following publications in which these poems first appeared, some in slightly different versions:

Arkansas Review: "To get to Cowlake"
Assaracus: "For what I assume is membership," "Jubilate," "Knowledge," and "Playground"
Borderlands: Texas Poetry Review: "Jewels of Opar"
Chattahoochee Review: "Saint's finger, Hill of Slane" and "Still"
Country Dog Review: "An old pew"
Crannóg: "Teanga na mbláthanna" [The language of flowers]
Harvard Gay and Lesbian Review: "Genealogy: unidentified man in a photograph"
Kakalak 2009: Anthology of Carolina Poets: "Scavenge"
Louisville Review: "Nest" [Green pecans litter the street]
Natural Bridge: "Aisling" and "Shark"
A Poetry Congeries, Connotation Press: An Online Artifact: "Nest" [Dark wings], "Nest" [Two buds], and "Dead"
Rattle: "Church camp, summer 1977"
The Recorder: Journal of the American Irish Historical Society: "Early morning, fortieth birthday," "Epithalamion," "Knowledge," "Lost islands," and "Star"
Salamander: "Tenantry"
Sawmill: "Possum"
South Carolina Review: "Family Bible"
Texas Poetry Calendar 2010: "Late spring, near Leakey, Texas"
Texas Poetry Calendar 2014: "Wings"
Yemassee: "Larval"

"Aisling" was also included in *The Book of Irish American Poetry from the Eighteenth Century to the Present* (Notre Dame, 2007).

"Among men" and "Wrestling / Fable with shag carpet and bean bag chairs" will be published in *Queer South* (Sibling Rivalry Press, 2014).

"Coon Island" is modeled on Seamus Heaney's "Mossbawn: Two Poems in Dedication."

"Counterpane,," which draws on and responds to chapter 4 of Herman Melville's *Moby Dick*, is chapter 4 of the *Remaking Moby Dick* project (2013-14) and appears online at: www.youtube.com/watch?v=zYrLf31KPWY.

"Early morning, fortieth birthday" also appears in *A Millennial Sampler of South Carolina Poetry* (Ninety-Six Press, 2005).

"Hammock" (part 1 of "Weekend) appeared as "Weekend" in *After Shocks: The Poetry of Recovery for Life-Shattering Events* (Sante Lucia Books, 2008).

"Inferno" will be in published *Grit Po: Rough South Poetry*, edited by Daniel Cross Turner and William Wright.

"Jubilate" was published as winner of the 2010 Atlanta Queer Lit Festival Broadside Poem contest; the poem also appears in *Collective Brightness: LGBTIQ Poets on Faith, Religion, and Spirituality* (Sibling Rivalry Press, 2013).

"Vacation Bible School" appears in *This Assignment Is So Gay: LGBTIQ Poets on the Art of Teaching* (Sibling Rivalry, 2013).

The author would like to express thanks to Kwame Dawes, Ray McManus, and Daniel Nathan Terry for their comments and suggestions on earlier versions of this book. Special thanks to Jessie Lendennie and Siobhán Hutson at Salmon, and also to Mitchell Lonas for the beautiful cover image.

Photo: Kristine Hartvigsen

Born and raised in rural Arkansas, ED MADDEN teaches at the University of South Carolina. He is the author of two books of poetry, *Signals*, which won the South Carolina Poetry Book Prize, and *Prodigal: Variations*, as well as the chapbook, *My Father's House*. His poems have appeared in *Poetry Ireland Review*, *Cyphers*, *Los Angeles Review*, and other journals, as well as in *Best New Poets 2007* and *The Book of Irish American Poetry* (Notre Dame, 2007). He has also published on Irish literature and culture in *Éire/Ireland*, the *Canadian Journal of Irish Studies*, and the *Irish University Review*. He is literary arts editor for the magazine, *Jasper*.